PRINTING PRACTICE
HANDWRITING
WORKBOOK FOR KIDS

JULIE HARPER

Printing Practice Handwriting Workbook for Kids

Copyright © 2016 by Julie Harper

Cover Design by Melissa Stevens
www.theillustratedauthor.net
Write. Create. Illustrate.

Children's Books > Education & Reference > Words & Language

Children's Books > Education & Reference > Education > Workbooks

ISBN 10: 1523776560

EAN 13: 978-1523776566

Table of Contents

Introduction

The goal of this workbook is to inspire kids' interest in learning and practicing print handwriting. Kids enjoy reading phrases like, "No grown-ups allowed," and sentences like, "Puppies like to play." Exercises like these help to make learning fun, whether in the classroom or at home.

This *Printing Practice Handwriting Workbook for Kids* focuses on writing letters, words, phrases, and sentences in print.

Three sections of this workbook help students develop their print writing skills in three parts:

- ✓ Part 1 focuses on tracing and copying letters, words, and short phrases.

- ✓ Part 2 consists of longer sentences. There is no tracing in Part 2.

- ✓ Part 3 provides short writing exercises.

May your students or children improve their handwriting skills and enjoy reading and writing these letters, words, phrases, and sentences.

Uppercase Alphabet

A B C D E F

G H I J K L

M N O P Q R

S T U V W X

Y Z

Lowercase Alphabet

a b c d e f

g h i j k l

m n o p q r

s t u v w x

y z

Part 1 Letters and Words

Part 1 instructions: First trace each letter, word, or short phrase and then copy it onto the blank line below.

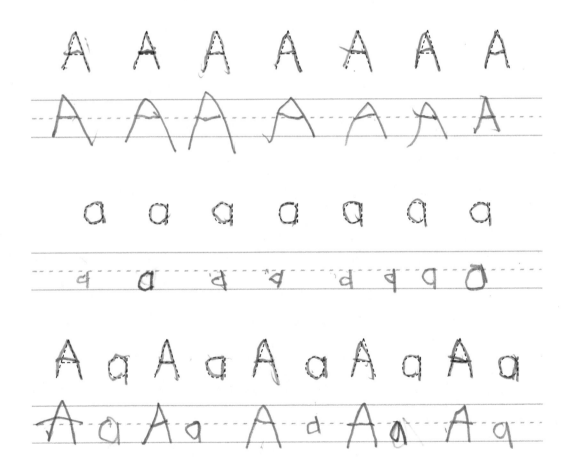

All aboard!

All aboard

Adorable ape

Adorable ape

Amazing acrobat

Amazing acrobat

Angry army ants

Angry army ants

Afraid of an alligator?

Afraid of an alligator?

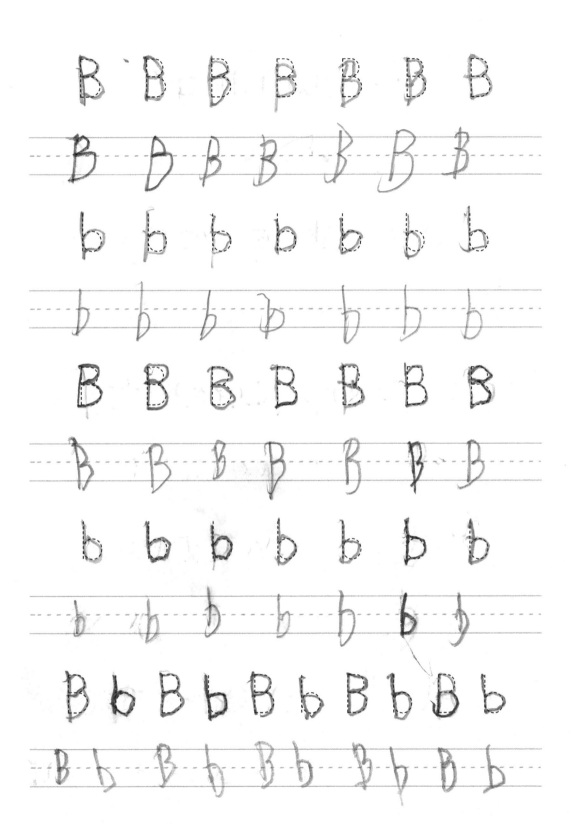

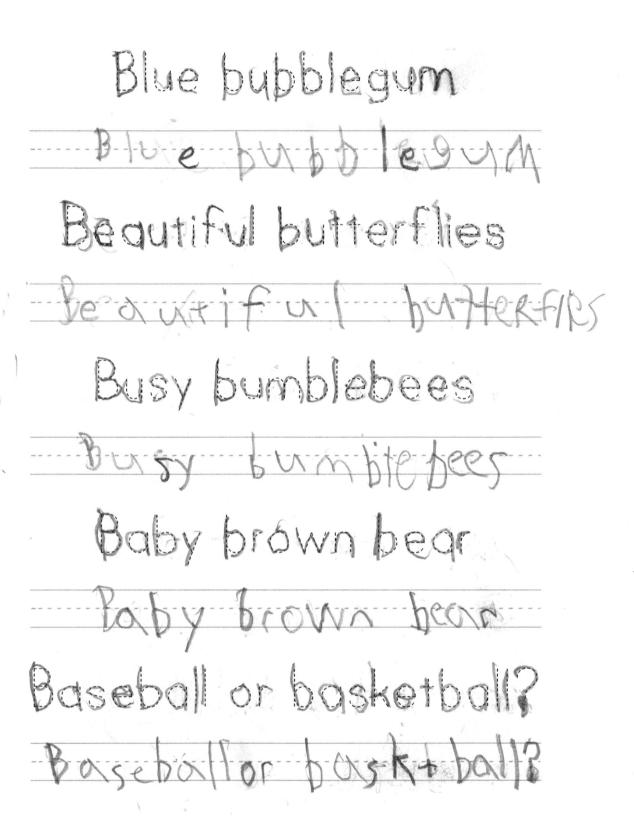

Blue bubblegum

Blue bubblegum

Beautiful butterflies

Beautiful butterflies

Busy bumblebees

Busy bumblebees

Baby brown bear

Baby brown bear

Baseball or basketball?

Baseball or basketball?

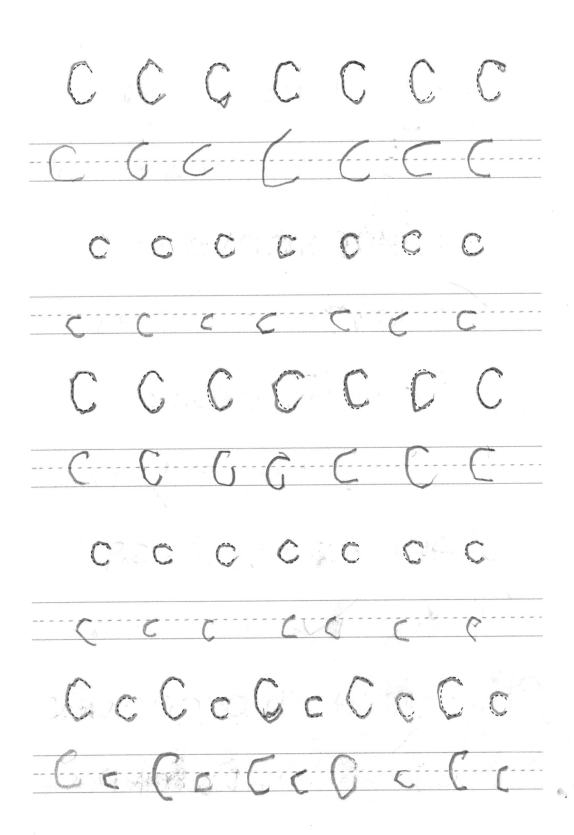

Curious cat

Curous cat

Clever coyote

Clever coyote

Colorful castle

Colorful castle

Checkers or chess?

Checkers or chess?

Chocolate chip cookies

Chocolate chip cookies

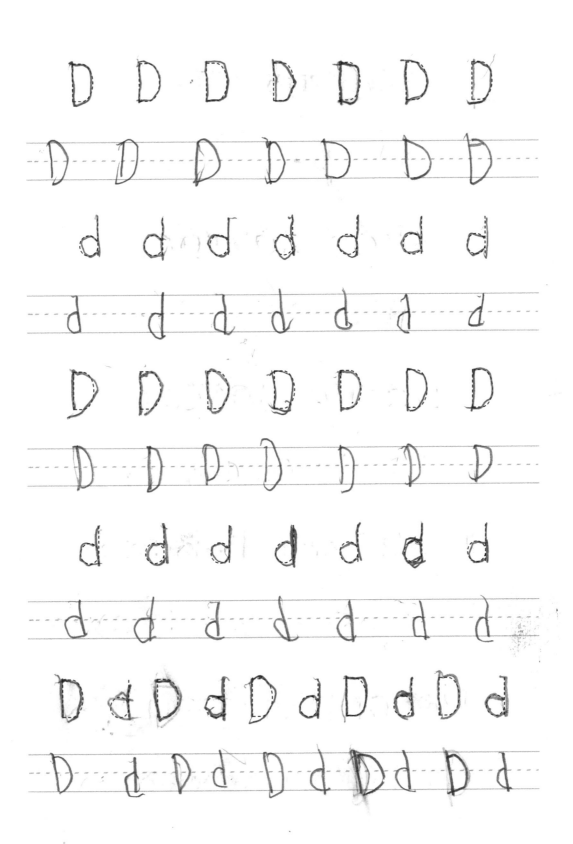

Delicious donut

Delicious donut

Drooling dog

Drooling dog

Daring dancer

Daring dancer

Draw doodlebugs

Draw doodlebugs

Delightful dream

Delightful dream

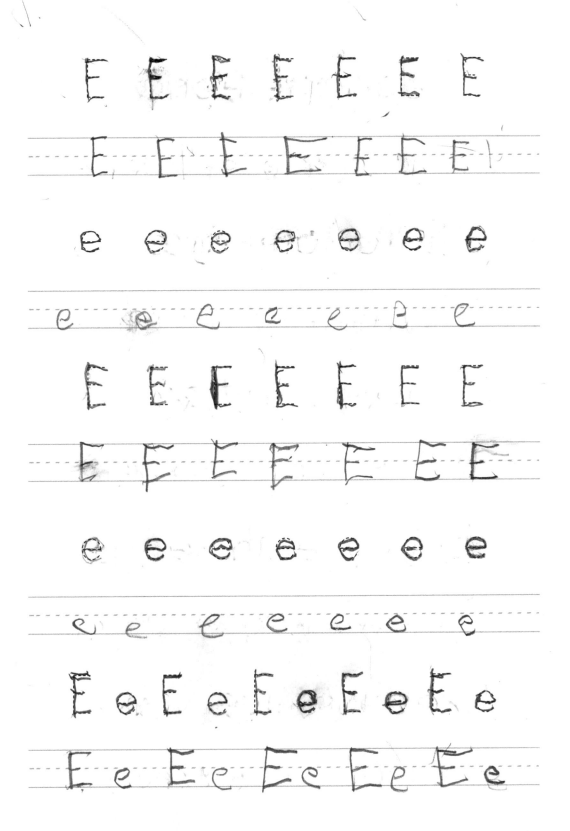

Elegant elephant

Elegant elephant

Entertaining elf

Entertaining elf

Extra effort

Extra effort

Eighty-eight eggs

Eighty eight eggs

Exercise every day

Exercise every day

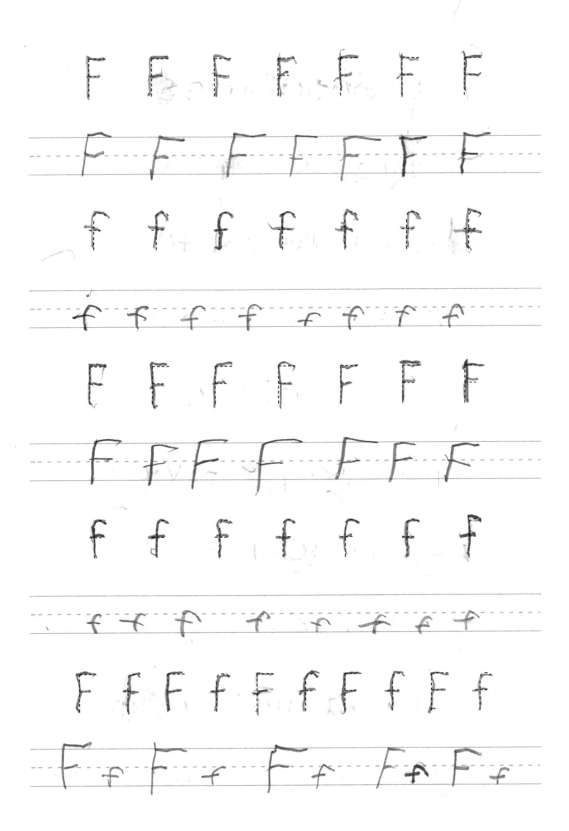

French fries

French fries

Favorite friend

Favorite friend

Fun festival

Fun festival

Flying fish

Flying fish

Fine family feast

Fine family feast

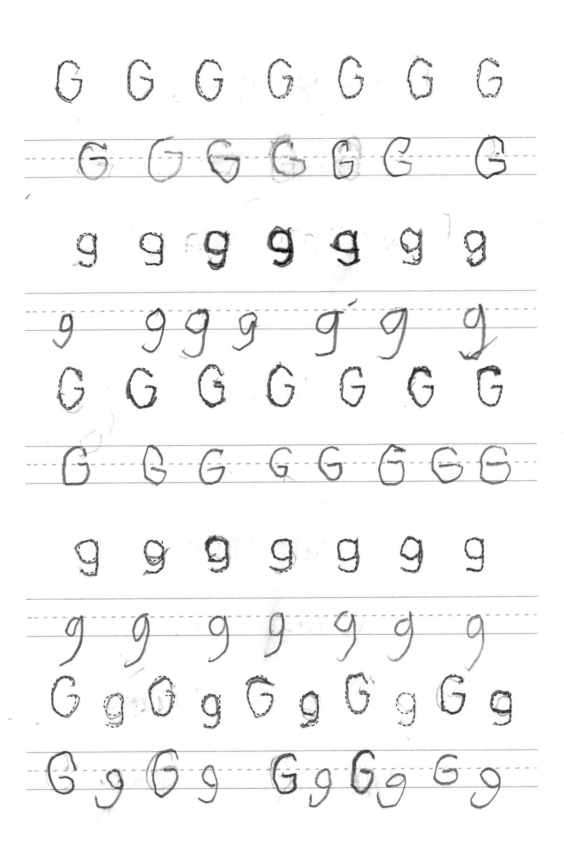

Goofy genius

Goofygenius

Guessing game

Guessing game

Grinning grandfather

Grinning grandfather

Giggling grandmother

Giggling grandmother

Gooey green gum

Gooey green gum

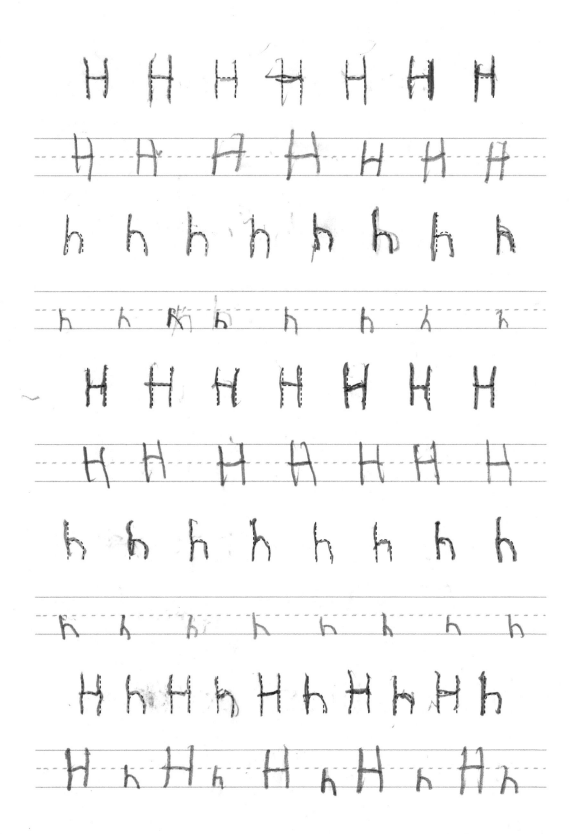

Hopping hare

Hopping hare

Hairy helmet

Hairy helmet

Heavenly harp

Heavenly harp

Have high hopes

Have high hope

Happy hippopotamus

Happy hippopotamus

I I I I I I I I I

i i i i i i i i i i

I I I I I I I I I

i i i i i i i i i

I i I i I i I i I i I i I i I i I i

Incredible idea

Infinite imagination

Invisible ingredient

Intelligent inchworm

Ice-cream in an igloo

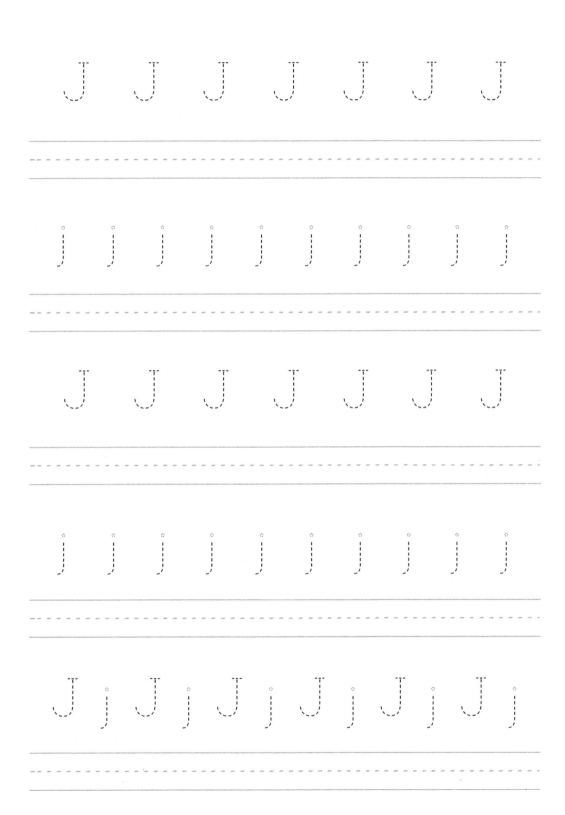

Jumping jacks

Just joking

Juggling jewelry

Jolly jester

Jazzy jeans

K K K K K K

k k k k k k k k

K K K K K K K

k k k k k k k k

K k K k K k K k

Knitting kitten

Kind king

Kidding koala

Kiss a kangaroo

Keep a kaleidoscope

L L L L L L L L

I I I I I I I I I I

L L L L L L L

I I I I I I I I I

L I L I L I L I L I L I L I L I

Love life

Like laughter

Loud lion

Long limousine

Lucky leprechaun

M M M M M M

m m m m m m

M M M M M M

m m m m m m

M m M m M m M m

Missed me!

Monkey mischief

Meet my mermaid

Mother, may I?

Miniature mouse

N   N   N   N   N   N   N

n   n   n   n   n   n   n

N   N   N   N   N   N   N

n   n   n   n   n   n   n

N n N n N n N n N n N n N n

No nonsense!

Nutty neighbor

Now or never!

Noisy nest

Naughty or nice?

O   O   O   O   O   O   O

o   o   o   o   o   o   o

O   O   O   O   O   O   O

o   o   o   o   o   o   o

O o O o O o O o O o O o O o

Odd one out

One o'clock

Orange overalls

One or the other

Octopus in the ocean

P P P P P P P

p p p p p p p

P P P P P P P

p p p p p p p

P p P p P p P p P p P p

Playful puppy

Purple princess

Private party

Proud papa

Pet polite pink pigs

Q   Q   Q   Q   Q   Q   Q

q   q   q   q   q   q   q

Q   Q   Q   Q   Q   Q   Q

q   q   q   q   q   q   q

Q q Q q Q q Q q Q q

Quick question

Quiet for the quiz

Quote the queen

Quack for a quarter

Quit quarrelling

R R R R R R R

r r r r r r r r

R R R R R R R

r r r r r r r r

Rr Rr Rr Rr Rr Rr Rr

Round rainbow

Runaway robots

Red ribbon

Remember our rooster

Racing rhinoceros

S   S   S   S   S   S   S

S   S   S   S   S   S   S   S

S   S   S   S   S   S   S

S   S   S   S   S   S   S

Ss Ss Ss Ss Ss Ss Ss

Smelly skunk

Sweet as sugar

Smiling student

Silly song

Sneaky snakes

T T T T T T T

t t t t t t t t t

T T T T T T T

t t t t t t t t t

T t T t T t T t T t T t

Tickle the teacher

That takes talent

Two tall tigers

Ten tiny turtles

Tiptoe to the toilet

Under an umbrella

Unusual underwear

Umpire uniform

Unique unicorn

Uncle on unicycle

V   V   V   V   V   V   V

V   V   V   V   V   V   V   V

V   V   V   V   V   V   V

V   V   V   V   V   V   V   V

V v V v V v V v V v

Velvet valentine

V is for victory

Very nice view

Vegetable van

Violet violin

Wacky welcome

Weeping walrus

Whispering women

Wonder why?

Wandering wolf

X-ray a fox

Xylophone

Sixty boxes

Exit the taxi

Fix the saxophone

Y Y Y Y Y Y Y

Y Y Y Y Y Y Y Y

Y Y Y Y Y Y Y

Y Y Y Y Y Y Y Y

Y y Y Y Y y Y y Y y

Yacking yak

Yummy yam

Yellow yarn

Yesterday

Yes, no, or maybe?

Z Z Z Z Z Z Z

Z Z Z Z Z Z Z Z

Z Z Z Z Z Z Z

Z Z Z Z Z Z Z Z

Z z Z z Z z Z z Z z

Zap the buzzer

Frozen pizza

Zip the zipper

Zebra at the zoo

Zoom through a zigzag

Part 2 Just Copy

Part 2 instructions: Just copy the words of these sentences onto the blank lines below. There is no tracing in Part 2.

Puppies like to play.

Kittens love yarn.

Hamsters exercise.

Go on a treasure hunt.

Find the map.

Search for clues.

X marks the spot.

Dig for a treasure.

Happy birthday!

Invite your friends.

Play party games.

Blow out the candles.

Open your presents.

Visit the circus.

Hello, ringmaster.

Watch acrobats fly.

Laugh at the clowns.

Enjoy the show.

Kick the ball.

Hop, skip, and jump.

Run fast and far.

Jump the highest.

Play hard.

Our secret clubhouse:

It's a treehouse.

No grown-ups allowed.

What's the password?

Devise great plans.

Go to an arcade.

Meet your friends.

Play arcade games.

Win prizes.

Play miniature golf.

We love movie night.

Can we get popcorn?

Who is the hero?

Will it be scary?

Cartoons are fun.

Fun in the snow!

Build a snowman.

Ski the slopes.

Don't forget your

scarf and mittens.

Build a sandcastle.

Throw a Frisbee.

Catch a wave.

Collect seashells.

Find a sand crab.

Ride a scooter.

Play at the park.

Skip rope with friends.

Play tag. You are it.

Pedal your bike.

Pick your sport.

Play for fun.

It takes teamwork.

Give it your all.

Cheer your team.

Sing a song.

Hit a high note.

Strum a guitar.

Play the piano.

Beat the drum.

What is your favorite

sport? Is it baseball,

gymnastics, football,

tennis, golf, soccer,

or something else?

Attend a pool party.

Splash in the water.

Swim fast.

Is diving allowed?

Play pool games.

It's a school day.

Ride the bus.

Get ready for class.

Learn something new.

Have fun at recess.

It's summer vacation!

Sleep in on Saturday.

Have fun with friends.

Play games outside.

Go on a road trip.

Ride a roller coaster.

Get soaked on a

water ride.

Eat delicious snacks.

Play carnival games.

Do you enjoy

campfires?

Roast a marshmallow.

Eat a hot dog.

Tell spooky stories.

What is your favorite

card game? Is it

crazy eights, solitaire,

hearts, spades, or

another game?

Coloring is fun.

Stay inside the lines.

Which colors go well

together? What's

your favorite color?

Take a trip to the zoo.

See bears, monkeys,

alligators, snakes,

lions, tigers, camels,

birds, and giraffes.

Be a good sport.

Play like a champion.

Own the moment.

Enjoy the game.

Shake hands after.

Have some candy.

Will it be chocolate,

licorice, caramels,

sugar cubes, taffy,

or another kind?

Scale a tall mountain.

Set up a tent.

Unroll a sleeping bag.

Sleep under the stars.

Count the stars.

Do you enjoy video

games? Do you prefer

puzzles, strategy,

teams, dancing, or

something else?

For a pet, would you

like a puppy, kitten,

hamster, parakeet,

parrot, snake, mouse,

or lizard?

Root for your team.

Eat a hotdog.

Cheer with the crowd.

Catch a foul ball.

Wear the team colors.

Tag, you're it.

You hide. I'll seek.

Kick the can.

Freeze tag!

Leap like a frog.

A full piggy bank is a

happy bank.

What will you save

your money for?

Keep saving.

The planets include

Mercury, Venus, Earth,

Mars, Jupiter, Saturn,

Uranus, and Neptune.

I feel bad for Pluto...

Take a rocket to the

moon. Ten, nine, eight,

seven, six, five, four,

three, two, one...

Blast off!

Take a trip to the

beach. Make a sand

castle. Splash in the

waves. Don't forget

to put on sunscreen.

It's time to exercise.

Do jumping jacks. Run

in place. Touch your

toes. Do somersaults

and cartwheels.

Care for a fairy tale?

Once upon a time...

Wish upon a star.

Dream big.

Live a happy ending.

Part 3 Writing Exercises

Part 3 instructions: Write answers to these questions in the space provided.

Exercise 1. List some types of pets.

_____
_____
_____

_____
_____
_____

Exercise 2. Which kind of pet is your favorite? Why?

_____
_____
_____

_____
_____
_____

_____
_____
_____

Exercise 3. Describe how a kitten looks.

_____

- -

_____

_____

- -

_____

Exercise 4. What do kittens like to do?

_____

- -

_____

_____

- -

_____

_____

- -

_____

Exercise 5. How do you take care of a kitten?

_____

- -

_____

_____

- -

_____

_____

- -

_____

Exercise 6. Describe how a puppy looks.

Exercise 7. What do puppies like to do?

Exercise 8. How do you take care of a puppy?

Exercise 9. List some toys that you like.

Exercise 10. Describe your favorite toy.

Exercise 11. Describe another toy that you like.

Exercise 12. List some games that you like.

Exercise 13. Describe your favorite game.

Exercise 14. Describe another game that you like.

Exercise 15. List some fun places that you could go.

Exercise 16. What would you do at an amusement park?

Exercise 17. What would you do at the beach?

Exercise 18. List animals that you could find at a zoo.

Exercise 19. Describe your favorite zoo animal.

Exercise 20. Describe another zoo animal.

Exercise 21. List some funny sounds (like zoink or mooooo).

Exercise 22. Describe something funny that you've seen.

Exercise 23. Describe something funny that you've heard.

Exercise 24. List some colors.

Exercise 25. Which is your favorite color. Why?

Exercise 26. Describe some things that are in your favorite color.

Exercise 27. List some things that you're good at.

_____

- -

_____

- -

_____

Exercise 28. Pick one. How do you know you're good at it?

_____

- -

_____

- -

_____

- -

_____

Exercise 29. Describe something that you wish you could do better.

_____

- -

_____

- -

_____

- -

_____

Exercise 30. List some hobbies.

Exercise 31. Describe your favorite hobby.

Exercise 32. Describe another hobby.

Exercise 33. List the title and author of your favorite book.

Exercise 34. What happens in the book?

Exercise 35. Why do you like the book?

Exercise 36. What is the name of your favorite movie?

Exercise 37. What happens in the movie?

Exercise 38. Why do you like the movie?

Exercise 39. List some kinds of food.

_____
- -
_____

_____
- -
_____

Exercise 40. Describe your favorite food.

_____
- -
_____

_____
- -
_____

_____
- -
_____

Exercise 41. Describe another food that you like.

_____
- -
_____

_____
- -
_____

_____
- -
_____

Exercise 42. List some cities that you might like to visit.

_____

- -

_____

- -

_____

Exercise 43. Describe a city that you've visited before.

_____

- -

_____

- -

_____

- -

_____

Exercise 44. Imagine a city that you'd like to visit. Describe it.

_____

- -

_____

- -

_____

- -

_____

Exercise 45. List some kinds of weather.

_____

- -

_____

_____

- -

_____

Exercise 46. Describe your favorite weather.

_____

- -

_____

_____

- -

_____

_____

- -

_____

Exercise 47. Describe your least favorite weather.

_____

- -

_____

_____

- -

_____

_____

- -

_____

Exercise 48. List some school subjects.

Exercise 49. Describe your favorite school subject.

Exercise 50. Describe another school subject.

Exercise 51. List some things you might see at a circus.

Exercise 52. What do clowns do at a circus?

Exercise 53. What do trapeze artists do at a circus?

Exercise 54. List some things you might find at a park.

Exercise 55. Describe something fun you can do at the park.

Exercise 56. Describe something else you can do at a park.

Exercise 57. List some things you might find in a garden.

Exercise 58. Describe things insects might do in a garden.

Exercise 59. Describe smells you might enjoy in a garden.

Exercise 60. Make up an imaginary creature.

Exercise 61. What might your imaginary creature do?

Exercise 62. What makes your imaginary creature special?

Exercise 63. Write something funny.

Exercise 64. Write something interesting.

Exercise 65. Write something happy.

Cursive Handwriting Practice Workbook for Boys

Cursive Handwriting Workbook for Girls

Julie Harper's Workbooks

www.wackysentences.com

Printing Practice:

- ✓ Printing Practice Handwriting Workbook for Girls.
- ✓ Printing Practice Handwriting Workbook for Boys.
- ✓ Tongue Twisters Printing Practice Writing Workbook.
- ✓ Print Uppercase and Lowercase Letters, Words, and Silly Phrases: Kindergarten and First Grade Writing Practice Workbook (Reproducible).
- ✓ Print Wacky Sentences: First and Second Grade Writing Practice Workbook (Reproducible).

Cursive Handwriting:

- ✓ Letters, Words, and Silly Phrases Handwriting Workbook (Reproducible): Practice Writing in Cursive (Second and Third Grade).
- ✓ Wacky Sentences Handwriting Workbook (Reproducible): Practice Writing in Cursive (Third and Fourth Grade).
- ✓ Cursive Handwriting Workbook for Kids.
- ✓ Cursive Handwriting Workbook for Girls.
- ✓ Cursive Handwriting Practice Workbook for Teens.
- ✓ Spooky Cursive Handwriting Practice Workbook.
- ✓ Cursive Handwriting Practice Workbook for Boys.

Reading & Writing:

- ✓ Reading Comprehension for Girls (48 Fun Short Stories).
- ✓ Wacky Stories (10 Short Stories for Kids).
- ✓ Wacky Creative Writing Assignments Workbook.

Made in the USA
Middletown, DE
01 June 2019